My First ACROSTIC

The South Of England

Edited by Jenni Bannister

First published in Great Britain in 2015 by:

Remus House
Coltsfoot Drive
Peterborough
PE2 9BF
Telephone: 01733 890066
Website: www.youngwriters.co.uk

Printed and bound in the UK by BookPrintingUK
Website: www.bookprintinguk.com

FOREWORD

Welcome, Reader!

For Young Writers' latest competition, My First Acrostic, we gave Key Stage 1 children nationwide the challenge of writing an acrostic poem on the topic of their choice.

Poetry is a wonderful way to introduce young children to the idea of rhyme and rhythm and helps learning and development of communication, language and literacy skills. The acrostic form is a great introduction to poetry, giving a simple framework for pupils to structure their thoughts while at the same time allowing more confident writers the freedom to let their imaginations run wild.

Here at Young Writers our aim is to encourage creativity in children and to inspire a love of the written word, so it's great to get such an amazing response, with some absolutely fantastic poems. This made it a tough challenge to pick the winners, so well done to **Nadia Hawley** who has been chosen as the best poet in this anthology.

Due to the young age of the entrants we have tried to include as many of the poems as possible. By giving these young poets the chance to see their work in print we hope to encourage their love of poetry and give them the confidence to continue with their creative efforts – I look forward to reading more of their poems in the future.

Jenni Bannister

Editorial Manager

CONTENTS

Eton Wick CE First School, Windsor

Heron Park Academy, Eastbourne

Kingswood Primary School, Tadworth

New Marston Primary School, Oxford

Oakfield Primary School, Southampton

Our Lady's Preparatory School, Crowthorne

St Bernadette's Catholic Primary School, Farnborough

St Erme with Trispen Community Primary School, Truro

The Baird Primary Academy, Hastings

Turners Hill CE Primary School, Crawley

Wildground Infant School, Southampton

THE POEMS

Summer

S un shining every day

U mbrella in the garden for shade

M aking sandcastles at the beach

M e and my family go on holiday

E ating barbecues and having parties

R ain comes and summer is over.

Sophie Mae Taylor (7)
Bedenham Primary School, Gosport

Summer

S ummer is for sun, sea and sand

U mbrellas shade you from the sun

M elting ice creams everywhere

M y daddy cooking on the barbecue

E veryone sunbathing on the beach

R ubbing suntan lotion on so I don't get burnt.

Lucas Field (6)
Bedenham Primary School, Gosport

1

Elizabeth Bailey

E njoying playing in the sun

L earning at school is lots of fun

I love playing with my friends

Z zzzzzz, sleeping helps me rest

A pples are juicy which I like to eat

B eware of the pips, I don't want to swallow

E lephants are my favourite animal

T humping through the town

H eading home, they go for a nice treat

B ouncing on the trampoline

A wards go to the one who jumps high

I like to fly high, be careful because

L unch might come up over

E veryone

Y ay, I am done.

Elizabeth Bailey (6)
Bedenham Primary School, Gosport

2

Lucy Kensall

L ovely Lucy
U sually happy, always smiling
C is for cool
Y ou are beautiful my mum says

K ind, always be kind
E ating pasta is my favourite
N eed my cuddles before bed
S trawberries are delicious
A frica is my favourite country
L ove playing with my friends
L ove playing with my toys.

Lucy Emma Kensall (6)
Bedenham Primary School, Gosport

Superhero

S is for saving the world

U is for united in a team

P is for the power they have

E is for the enemies they fight

R is for running, Flash is the fastest

H is for help that they give each other

E is for energy, they all have lots

R is for remember to always help

O is for origins stories.

Ruben Storey (7)
Bedenham Primary School, Gosport

Nanny

N anny is awesome

A lways silly with us

N ever gets cross

N ight-times at Nanny's are best

Y ummy treats are at her house.

Talan Hartley Cooper (6)
Bedenham Primary School, Gosport

Sharif El Sayed

S is for silly

H is for happy

A is for action man

R is for reading, I like to read

I is for identity and intelligence

F is for fantastically friendly

E is for entertaining

L is for listening

S is for spelling, the best in the class

A is for awesome

Y is for young and yelling

E is for educated

D is for descriptive.

Sharif El Sayed (6)
Bedenham Primary School, Gosport

5

Fairies

F ly really high with big wings

A fairy is very magical

I think a fairy makes dreams come true

R eally good at doing magic

I think fairies are very special

E veryone has to believe

S oft, beautiful clothes.

Maisie-Ann Mitchell (5)
Bedenham Primary School, Gosport

Olivia

O n summer days I like to play

L ike ice cream

I n winter it snows

V elvet flowers I like to smell

I like my family

A kind girl like me

I am amazing at art

S o in winter I like to play

G ood girls like me get a good job

R ainy days I like to play

E at good food or you won't live

A nimals and nature are awesome!

T rees and oxygen help you live.

Olivia Onifade (7)
Bedenham Primary School, Gosport

My Favourite Game

M ining is fun

I like building, mining and stuff

N ever dig straight down

E nchantment table is good

C rafting is best for caves

R are diamonds are hard to find

A fter dark mobs come out

F orests are hard to find

T onight I will be mining.

Noah Uniacke (7)
Bedenham Primary School, Gosport

The Seaside

S izzling sausages on the barbecue

E xcited children eating their lunch

A nchor dropping from a cruise ship

S limy starfish stuck to a rock

I ce cream is melting in the scorching sun

D elicious hot dogs with yellow mustard

E dible shrimp on the seabed below.

Emery Whittle-Jamal (6)
Boundary Oak School, Fareham

The Seaside

S andy yellow beach

E xploring the seashore looking for pearls

A crab is walking sideways

S ea creatures are amazing

I went on holiday to the seaside

D elicious soft chocolate ice cream

E dible crabs to cook on a barbecue.

Tom Wybourne (7)
Boundary Oak School, Fareham

The Seaside

S parkly water shining in the sun

E ating ice cream, my favourite flavour is chocolate

A mazing urchins wobbling in the water like jelly

S parkly seaweed wiggling silly

I like sandcastles

D olphins surfing loop-the-loop

E ating sandy sandwiches.

Sofia Dewsbury (6)
Boundary Oak School, Fareham

9

The Seaside

S hining fish in the beautiful sea

E ating fish is lush

A beautiful dolphin diving in the sea

S harp crabs in the sea

I magine a shark next to me

D ead fish washing up on the shore

E ating chips in my chair.

James Wilby-Lopez (6)
Boundary Oak School, Fareham

The Seaside

S andy seagulls rushing through the air

E ating fish

A mazing crabs on the sand

S lippery jellyfish in my bucket

I saw fancy fish

D iving for treasure

E ven beautiful starfish!

Amelie Swarbrick (6)
Boundary Oak School, Fareham

Stone Cold Steve Austin

S uper (he is one of the best wrestlers of all time)

T errific (he held the WWE title)

O riginal (he invented The Stunner)

N oisy (he yells, he calls, he cheers and he screams)

E nergetic (fast and speedy)

C ool (as a cheetah)

O utstanding (he is strong and powerful)

L ucky (he wins a lot of matches)

D azzling (uniform)

S porty (he does a lot of hard work)

T ough (he picked someone up)

E legant (like a tiger)

V ery kind (to his fans)

E ffective (beating his opponents)

A ctive (sporty and speedy)

U nique (he rubs his opponent's head and rubs it on the floor)

S ensitive (he cares about his fans)

T erribly impressive

I ncredible moves

N eat and unique.

Brandon Robert Marchant (8)
Brackenbury Primary School, Portslade

Ender Dragon

E xplosive (he throws exploding balls)

N aughty (tries to kill you)

D angerous (tries to destroy its enemy)

E xtreme evil (he likes murder and destruction)

R ude (shooting and disturbing)

D emon (he lives in the most dangerous place in the world)

R apid (shooter)

A nnoying (you all the time)

G reat (destroyer)

O h, oh (he is a big, bad guy)

N ightmare (he defeats you in every way).

River Conrad Banks (8)
Brackenbury Primary School, Portslade

Triple H

T ough Triple H

R ipper river

I mpressive interesting moves

P owerful person

L ucky life

E xtremely evil

H ated horror!

Jamie Snow (8)
Brackenbury Primary School, Portslade

Blaze

B ig pain follows you everywhere

L aughing when people die

A dores killing people

Z aps you on fire

E nergised because he goes everywhere.

Callum Huntingford (9)
Brackenbury Primary School, Portslade

The Undertaker

T hunder and lightning

H ulk (strong and powerful)

E pic (at everything

U ndertakes to do the chokeslam

N aughty (he tricks people)

D eath (he always comes back to life)

E nergetic (he never gets tired)

R ipper (he rips up people's dreams)

T ough (because he trains a lot)

A ngelic (like a mean angel)

K ick (start the motorbike)

E legant (like a butterfly)

R ed (flaming up).

Max Elliott (9)
Brackenbury Primary School, Portslade

Jon

J oyful (because his smile is lit up and so massive it goes
round the back of his head)

O ptimistic (because he never gives up)

N ickname (Sky Constructor).

Dylan Pearce (9)
Brackenbury Primary School, Portslade

Hungry Bats

B ony wings
A ble to catch moths
T earing the moths. *Chomp! Chomp!*

George Sanderson (5)
Breamore CE Primary School, Fordingbridge

Super Bat

B ats have a white line on their backs
A dorable and cute
T iny, scary and dazzling.

Georgina Wilson (6)
Breamore CE Primary School, Fordingbridge

Ella's Bats

B ony claws
A mazing big wings
T eeth are sharp.

Ella Bellini (6)
Breamore CE Primary School, Fordingbridge

Writing About Bats

B ony wings
A ble to catch a moth
T hirsty, thick, thin, thundering.

Emeka Onyewuchi (5)
Breamore CE Primary School, Fordingbridge

Bats Are Deadly

B ats are silent but deadly
A ttracting their prey in a flash
T racking and tearing their prey
S cratching their claws like a cat.

Oliver Charlesworth (7)
Breamore CE Primary School, Fordingbridge

About Bats

B lack, beautiful, brave and very deadly
A dorable and fluffy like a pussycat
T earing teeth like a dinosaur
S cary but tiny.

Katie Drake
Breamore CE Primary School, Fordingbridge

Bats

B eautiful, silent, deadly

A ble to catch their prey easily

T errific and super fast

S ome bats are like a rocket across the night sky.

Rafe Thomas Munster (7)
Breamore CE Primary School, Fordingbridge

Bats

B ats sneak out at night because they hate the terrible daylight

A bat is furry on its tummy but skinny everywhere else

T hey are beautiful but deadly

S ome are brown like squelchy dark mud.

Tristan Prinsloo (6)
Breamore CE Primary School, Fordingbridge

Bat Poem

B eautiful but bony

A lert for the moths

T eeth can slay a tiny moth in just a second

S urprisingly their skin is like melted chocolate.

Jack Godden (6)
Breamore CE Primary School, Fordingbridge

Batty Batty Bat Bat

B rave bats track at night
A lerted a moth!
T hundering like a brave knight
S neaky little bats.

Emily Bechter
Breamore CE Primary School, Fordingbridge

Bats Are Amazing

B ony but brave, sneaky and brown
A ttacks its prey straightaway!
T earing its prey with its razor-sharp teeth, it swoops like a
blazing bird.

William Sanderson (7)
Breamore CE Primary School, Fordingbridge

My Bat Poem

B ats bundle like ghosts ready to tear moths to smithereens
A gile and fierce like a Spitfire hunting the enemy
T earing and tumbling, swooping and hanging
S lick and fast.

Joffe Anderson (7)
Breamore CE Primary School, Fordingbridge

Deadly Bats In The World

B ats are black and terrifying

A mazing bats eat fruit

T hey hang upside down in caves.

Ekene Onyewuchi (6)
Breamore CE Primary School, Fordingbridge

Minibeast

M arvellous and interesting minibeasts

I 've found an insect in my garden

N aughty and cross wasps are stinging

I think I've been stung by a hornet

B eat hornets because they sting

E ating butterflies and hornets

A long with the bees you go

S top! There's a hornet

T op of the insect list is hornets.

Amelia Geraghty-Bellingham (6)
Compton & Up Marden CE School, Chichester

Butterflies

B utterflies are beautiful

U p goes the butterfly

T he butterfly's wings are beautiful

T iny butterflies

E xciting butterflies

R ather exciting butterflies

F unny butterflies

L ittle butterflies

I like butterflies

E ating butterflies

S pecial butterflies.

Joshua Lewis (6)
Compton & Up Marden CE School, Chichester

Minibeast

M ummy snails

I n the garden

N asty wasps

I nteresting bees

B ees buzzing around

E ating nectar

A mazing

S ea snails

T iny ladybirds

S ome ladybirds were buzzing around.

Ben Watson (6)
Compton & Up Marden CE School, Chichester

Snails And Slugs

S limy snails

N ice slugs

A tiny slug and snail

I nky slugs and snails

L ovely slugs and snails

S hells are curly

A mazing snails

N ever very fast snails

D ancing snails

S lithering snails

L eaf with a snail on

U nder leaves you'll see snails

G reedy snails

S ticky slugs.

Chloe Tutt (6)
Compton & Up Marden CE School, Chichester

Butterflies

B eautiful butterflies

U p flies a butterfly

T he butterflies fly around

T he butterflies are sleeping

E ating leaves

R eally interesting

F rolicking butterflies

L ike the honeybees

I nteresting

E xcited butterflies

S mall butterflies.

Caitlin Vance (6)
Compton & Up Marden CE School, Chichester

Ladybirds

L ove lying

A mini ladybird

D ancing on a daisy

Y ou need ladybirds

B lack and red ladybirds

I nteresting ladybirds

R unning ladybirds

D rumming ladybirds

S ecure ladybirds.

Ella Mae Roxburgh (7)
Compton & Up Marden CE School, Chichester

Minibeasts

M inibeasts are cool!

I 've seen one before

N ever hurt them

I ncredible minibeasts

B est in the world

E xtra exciting

A nts are interesting

S lithering snails

T arantulas spinning webs

S limy slugs.

Harry Hudson (7)
Compton & Up Marden CE School, Chichester

Butterflies

B uzzing butterflies

U p in the air

T hey make the world look pretty

T iger butterfly is flying in the air

E ating a lot of pollen

R eally interesting important butterflies

F ascinating fast butterfly

L ovely butterfly

I nteresting amazing butterflies

E very butterfly is gorgeous

S mall butterflies.

Scott Peter Simpson (7)
Compton & Up Marden CE School, Chichester

Ladybirds

L adybirds are interesting

A pretty ladybird

D ippy ladybirds

Y ippee ladybirds

B aby ladybird

I gloo ladybird

R unning ladybird

D rumming ladybird

S low ladybird.

Amber Oeder (6)
Compton & Up Marden CE School, Chichester

Minibeast

M inibeasts are marvellous

I nteresting insects

N ew nasty maggots are noisy

I nteresting insects

B ugs are big

E arwigs are not enormous

A pples as a house

S piders are super

T errible insects

S illy special insects.

William Ponsonby (7)
Compton & Up Marden CE School, Chichester

Minibeasts

M arvellous minibeasts

I 've found a butterfly

N asty naughty spider

I love butterflies

B ig spiders, little spiders

E nter all the insects

A nts, caterpillars, snails and slugs

S illy slugs

T iny creatures

S mall spider.

Hollie Treagus (7)
Compton & Up Marden CE School, Chichester

Marvellous Minibeasts

M inibeasts are interesting

I 've found a beetle

N ew butterflies in the cities

I have never seen a moth like this

B eautiful bees in a jar

E at pollen and soil

A te a leaf at 7 o'clock

S nails rolling in the school and village

T iny monsters in the garden

S melly slugs and snails.

Jasper Bathmaker (7)
Compton & Up Marden CE School, Chichester

Centipedes

C rawling crazy centipedes!

E normous and scary

N ever too short, never too long

T hey squirm and wiggle until they're tired

I mportant centipedes

P erfectly camouflaged!

E very centipede is perfect

D on't think they're rude because they're not

E njoy playing with other centipedes

S ome are kind and happy.

Thaila Wyatt (7)
Compton & Up Marden CE School, Chichester

Butterflies

B eautiful tiny butterflies

U p, up in the air

T iny teeny weeny butterflies

T iger butterflies are flapping in the sky

E ating pollen

R eally rubbish butterflies

F ascinating fliers butterflies

L ovely liking butterflies

I 've found an incredible butterfly!

E very butterfly is gorgeous

S mall silly butterflies.

Sophie Reid (7)
Compton & Up Marden CE School, Chichester

Dragonflies

D ragonflies are interesting

R eally fast butterfly

A ll their wings are see-through

G rip on dragonfly

O n the pond

N ormal dragonfly

F lying dragonfly

L ovely and nervous

I n the pond they like to fly

E nter all the dragonflies

S illy dragonfly.

Ellie Mobey (7)
Compton & Up Marden CE School, Chichester

Small Snails

S nails are slimy

M oist snail

A snail is angry

L ogs fall on the snail

L eaves fall on the snail

S limy snail leaving a trail

N aughty snail

A snail has a shell

I t's a funny snail

L umpy snail

S olid snail.

Elliott Pearce (5)
Compton & Up Marden CE School, Chichester

Minibeasts

M oths are cute but they come out at night

I nsects are so interesting and so great

N ow I love minibeasts so much

I n the cocoon there are some caterpillars

B uzzy bees flying from flower to flower

E arthworms and slugs enjoying the mud

A mazing sight of minibeasts

S nails leave a trail

T arantulas are scary for people

S ee lots of minibeasts!

Terri-Jayne Dysell (6)
Compton & Up Marden CE School, Chichester

Deep Sea Dumbo

D eep water device
E lectronic ears
E very fish bows down to me
P uts its eyes on its prey

S cary sight!
E els attract many fish but not me!
A mazing eyes

D angling tentacles
U sually counts on me
M ostly, everybody
B ill the vampire squid is my worst nightmare
O h no! I've got to go, bye-bye!

Ben Cooper (7)
Esher CE (A) Primary School, Esher

36

Cute Terrapins

C ute sea creatures

U nder the sea where you find them

T errapins are usually identical

E xcellent is their second name

T hey are my favourite sea creatures

E very one of them is lovely!

R eally everyone should like them

R arely they ever sleep!

A tortoise and a turtle look just like a terrapin

P robably everyone likes a terrapin

I ncredibly small!

N ormally they live in large groups

S inging about them makes me happy.

Matilda Louise Stanfield (7)
Esher CE (A) Primary School, Esher

Jude Fox

J ude Fox is my name

U sually I play football at the weekend

D oes anything he can to help his friends

E verything to help my friends

F riendly

O f course I like my friends

X is the hardest one.

Jude Fox (7)
Esher CE (A) Primary School, Esher

Baby Arthur

B est baby

A bsolutely great

B est brother ever

Y ippee he's so great

A great player

R unning, trying to keep up with me

T rains are his favourite toy

H e loves my toys

U p high! I lift him

R ufus loves him.

Rufus Shilington (6)
Esher CE (A) Primary School, Esher

Shark

S o terrifying
H ates eating grass
A s big as a crocodile
R acing trying to eat fish
K ing of the sea.

Jare Salami (7)
Esher CE (A) Primary School, Esher

Jumping Jellyfish

J iggling up
E agerly dangerous
L olly slipper
L ightly pink
Y o-yo like
F at and thin
I wouldn't touch them if I were you!
S hhhh, they will sting you
H umph! I am very boring.

Tom O'Brien (6)
Esher CE (A) Primary School, Esher

Seahorses!

S ea-splashing creatures living in the sea

E at lovely seaweed

A t midday when the sun's at its hottest they play

H orses do not have wings but we do!

O ften they change colour when they're scared

R eally often we are fast

S eahorses play all day

E ach seahorse fights for the girls.

Amelie Grace Bruce (7)
Esher CE (A) Primary School, Esher

Dogfish

D ogfish

O ctopus, I am not like an octopus

G o buy me some swimming goggles mate

F ins, soggy fins

I 'm super

S hare my food, no way!

H i, my name is Mr Dogfish but I've got to go.

Teddy Rawlinson (7)
Esher CE (A) Primary School, Esher

Dolphin And Starfish

D own the dark, dark sea

O ctopus hate me

L eaps in the water

P retty good swimmers

H ere's a shiny animal

I n the ocean you find me

N o people have ever found me.

Caitlin Annie Weihs (7)
Esher CE (A) Primary School, Esher

Monty My Pet

M onty is marvellous

O pens stair gates

N ibbler he is

T akes my breakfast

Y ummy treats he takes from me

M onty is funny

Y um, he is always hungry

P uppy he is

E ars he has

T asty food he loves.

Bethany Emily Worthington (7)
Esher CE (A) Primary School, Esher

41

Seahorse

S eahorses have curly tails

E ach time you see me I look like a dragon

A seahorse like me can uncurl its tail

H orses can't though

O ctopuses can

R ocks can be lifted by seahorses

S eahorses can make squeaky noises

E ach time I squeak the sea rattles.

Poppy Davidson (6)
Esher CE (A) Primary School, Esher

Babies

B rilliant

A nnoying babies

B abies are cute

I mpossible to not like babies

E xciting when one arrives

S uper babies are cool.

Beth Gatward (7)
Esher CE (A) Primary School, Esher

Predator Alert

A nxious predator

N asty spotlight

G reat meat eater

L ives in dark murky water

E normous teeth

R ummaging fins

F ears carnivores

I n cold waters

S himmering fish

H elping with other schools.

Lucien Nicholas Sorgendal (7)
Esher CE (A) Primary School, Esher

Rudolph

R ed nose

U seful

D elightful

O f course I love Rudolph

L oving Rudolph is good

P erhaps Rudolph is magical

H elpful.

Felix Harper (7)
Esher CE (A) Primary School, Esher

Coco

C oco is my cat
O n my bed asleep
C oco is cute
O f course I love Coco.

Tom Royan (6)
Esher CE (A) Primary School, Esher

Roisy

R unning is fun
O f course she is wonderful
I think she is marvellous
S illy dog
Y oung she is.

Jessica Morgan (6)
Esher CE (A) Primary School, Esher

Lego Bricks

L ego is better than school

E stelle is a Lego fan

G reen Lego bricks can be grass

O range Lego trousers can be pulled off

B ricks that are Lego can be different

R eally popular Lego bricks

I am a fan of Lego

C ome and make Lego with me

K ids can make Lego

S nakes can be Lego.

Max Webb (7)
Esher CE (A) Primary School, Esher

Spring

S piders crawl on the floor

P eople eat food

R ising of the sun

I can drive a car

N ick can ride a bike

G reen grass.

Musa Malik (6)
Eton Wick CE First School, Windsor

Spring

S leep
P retty daisies
R ain
I spy
N ice weather
G row.

Ruby Camandona-Philips (5)
Eton Wick CE First School, Windsor

Spring

S unshine is a nice type of weather
P lanting plants is fun
R ains a lot in spring
I ncredible animals come out
N ew plants come up
G ardening, growing plants.

Zoë Hibbert
Eton Wick CE First School, Windsor

Spring

S un is my favourite weather
P arties are my favourite thing
R iding on my bike is my favourite thing
I like it, it is so, so, so sunny
N ice when my friends come to my house
G reat when I go to the running park.

Ellie Macnamara (5)
Eton Wick CE First School, Windsor

Spring

S unny sunshine
P lants are perfect
R unny rain
I nside it's too hot but outside it's OK
N ever step on new plants
G rass grows a lot.

Tinashe Tafara Zichawo (6)
Eton Wick CE First School, Windsor

47

Spring

S ee the sight of the sun

P ink blossom

R ake the lawn

I t's the great time in spring

N eat spring

G reen grass is sparkling.

Simon Hayward (6)
Eton Wick CE First School, Windsor

Spring

S ometimes it's sunny in spring

P lanting plants

R eally nearly ready plants

I n spring in England flowers grow

N ormal rain racing down

G reen grass is everywhere.

Zaryab Shakir (6)
Eton Wick CE First School, Windsor

Spring

S quirrels are in the sunshine

P lants are pretty always

R ain is pointing down on the floor

I nsects come out in spring

N uts drop from trees

G reen grass is everywhere.

Tehya Ruci (5)
Eton Wick CE First School, Windsor

Spring

S unny sunshine

P retty plants

R adishes grow in spring

I gloos melt in spring

N odding daffodils

G oats eat in spring.

Luca Moston (6)
Eton Wick CE First School, Windsor

Spring

S un is lovely weather

P eople like playing in the pretty park

R iding on a pretty horse

I am playing on the green

N ice skill Harvey

G reat flip everyone.

Billy-Dean Lillywhite (6)
Eton Wick CE First School, Windsor

Spring

S leepy spider on a web

P retty pennies in spring

R ocking rabbits in spring and red robins

I nspiring plants in spring

N ew plants in spring

G reat plants in this season.

Phoebe Farmer (5)
Eton Wick CE First School, Windsor

Spring

S un
P retty flowers
R ock star
I nsects
N et for fish
G irl walking.

Arviene Chatha (5)
Eton Wick CE First School, Windsor

Spring

S pring is a lovely season
P eople might go on the trampoline
R ain might come in spring
I t is windy
N ever eat Shredded Wheat
G rass is very long.

Riley Martin (5)
Eton Wick CE First School, Windsor

Spring

S unny sky

P laying on the beach

R ed flowers

I am ready for my birthday

N ever touch sharp knives

G reen grass sparkles in the morning.

Tabitha Catherine Middleton (6)
Eton Wick CE First School, Windsor

Spring

S unshine

P lanting plants on a farm

R ed squirrels collecting nuts

I nsects hibernating

N ice weather in spring

G reen grass.

Amelia Moran (6)
Eton Wick CE First School, Windsor

Spring

S un comes in spring

P lanting all the plants

R ain makes plants grow

I nsects creep in spring

N ice weather in spring

G rowing plants is fun.

Mia Ridley (6)
Eton Wick CE First School, Windsor

Spring

S pring is fun

P ine cones are beautiful

R abbits are cute

I t's brilliant in spring

N uts fall off the trees

G reat, rabbits come out.

Harvey Rising (5)
Eton Wick CE First School, Windsor

Slug

S limy slug crawling around the house

L ittle baby slug and it was tiny

U gly slug, it was big and heavy

G reedy slug.

Freddie Prodger (7)

Heron Park Academy, Eastbourne

Ladybird

L ittle ladybird on a brown dark tree

A sticky ladybird walking on a green leaf

D angerous ladybird fell in a trash bin

Y ummy leaf fell in a hole

B umpy log went into a river

I got out said the ladybird, oh no!

R ivers lead to the sea. I saw a scaly leaf

D ragonfly saw ladybird.

Tariq Houri (7)

Heron Park Academy, Eastbourne

Slug

S limy slug on a stick
L ittle slug is eating apple
U nderneath the plant pot
G reedy slug eating apple.

Alfie Micheal Steven Nicholas (7)
Heron Park Academy, Eastbourne

Magnificent Minibeast

M agnificent minibeasts are so scary
I nsects like tarantulas are so hairy
N ever have I seen so many
I ncredible worms sold for a penny
B uzzing bees be careful they can sting you
E xtraordinary spiders can cast webs and they can shout boo!
A ladybird is spotty
S potty and dotty
T he ladybird is stinging because it can fly.

Chloe Mainstone (6)
Heron Park Academy, Eastbourne

Minibeast

M illipedes eating cucumber

I t left a bit of slime on my face

N ice scaly millipedes in a tree house

I can see the park

B e best at riding bikes

E at your dinner

A m I tiny?

S ee that spider

T iny ants.

Summer Tomlinson (7)
Heron Park Academy, Eastbourne

Minibeast

M y slug is slithering along a stick

I pick him up and put him in his cage

N ever again I did say

I t left slime all over my hand

B ad-tempered and moody

E at this it is healthy for you little slug

A ll around me there are slugs eating all the leaves

S piders casting webs in the dark gloomy night

T wo filthy slugs eating juicy apples in the sun.

Brooke Cavalier (7)
Heron Park Academy, Eastbourne

Minibeasts

M inibeasts are crawling around

I n a dark black hole a snail lives

N aughty spiders casting webs

I can see a naughty slug in my garden

B ees are buzzing around the hive

E ating a scrumptious leaf

A snail is as slow as a slug

S low snails

T asty cabbage

S limy slugs slithering.

Olivia Spinks (7)
Heron Park Academy, Eastbourne

Marvellous Minibeasts

M arvellous minibeasts are all around

I n ponds, trees and underground

N asty bugs flying in the air

I n soil under rocks and in your hair

B eautiful buzzing honeybee

E very time you eat your tea

A lthough there is a cute one that I know

S lides along so slow

T hat leaves a trail wherever they go.

Jessica Jane Crighton (7)
Heron Park Academy, Eastbourne

Minibeasts

M inibeasts are so small and tiny you get squashed

I n a spooky old house it's spooky

N aughty minibeasts eating some food in a garden

I n a garden yummy food of cabbage

B uzzing bees working, do not touch or get stung

E ating a scrumptious delicious carrot

A s a caterpillar turning into a beautiful butterfly

S lugs and snails are slow as a caterpillar

T ea is good as a carrot to drink

S nail is slow as a slug.

Samir Jurgelas (7)
Heron Park Academy, Eastbourne

Worm

W orms digging in the mud

O ut the plums they peep

R aindrops falling to the ground

M ushrooms become homes all around.

Taylor John Barker (7)
Heron Park Academy, Eastbourne

Minibeast

M inibeasts are small

I n a dark cave was a snail

N aughty ladybug in a cave

I n the cave all the minibeasts are gathering

B irds were catching worms

E arwigs are brown and fast

A nts are fast like a gizmo

S nails are slow as a caterpillar

T iny small caterpillar in a cave.

Bethany Fitches (7)
Heron Park Academy, Eastbourne

Worm

W orms dig in the ground

O ver plums and munching pears

R ound and round thinking the orchard is theirs

M uddled and jumbled they tumble to the ground.

Ellis Davids (7)
Heron Park Academy, Eastbourne

Butterfly

B eautiful patterned wings like petals falling in the breeze
U nique in their own way
T heir patterns are so pretty
T hey are an egg at first then turn into a caterpillar
E at! Eat! Eat! That's what they do
R eady to fly up in the sky that's so blue
F luttering onto sweet-smelling flowers
L ovely butterflies flying around
Y ou know they're so pretty.

Ruby McGurk-Balfour (7)
Heron Park Academy, Eastbourne

Marvellous Minibeasts

S lippery, slimy and so slow
N o birds eating this home
A home that protects me
I n my safe home
L ick my lips, food's coming.

Charley Woodgate (7)
Heron Park Academy, Eastbourne

Ant And Snail

A nts are fast and small and inside out

N o ant is clean and big

T he ant is silly and bony

S nail is slow and small

N o snail is a slug

A snail is slow and slimy

I am safe because of my shell

L ike the snail, I am slow.

Zayn Wood (7)
Heron Park Academy, Eastbourne

Flies And Snails

S nails are very slow and slimy

N o eating my body

A snail on a mountain

I am small

L ovely body

F lies can fly

L ittle flies try to fly

Y oung flies.

Nicolas Niemirow (6)
Heron Park Academy, Eastbourne

Ant

A ngry ant

N ever alone

T errified of humans.

Harley Romanis (7)

Heron Park Academy, Eastbourne

Snail

S nails are slimy

N o eating my shell

A snail is slow

I am a slimy snail

L ovely shell.

Mya Graham (7)

Heron Park Academy, Eastbourne

Animals

S lippery, silly and slow
N obody step on their heads
A shell to keep warm and cosy
I am warm
L onely with nobody.

Kelly-Anne Reid (6)
Heron Park Academy, Eastbourne

Snail

S lippery and slimy snail
N o stepping on the snails
A snail has teeth on its tongue
I feel safe in my shell
L ovely and lonely snail!

Alfie Moore (7)
Heron Park Academy, Eastbourne

Snails

S lippery and slimy
N apping all day
A really slow snail
I love the ground
L ove hiding in my shell.

Amy Shepherd (7)
Heron Park Academy, Eastbourne

Minibeasts

S caly, slimy, slow and slippery shell
N ice shell
A slow snail
I am safe in my shell
L iving in my shell.

Adrian Babowski (7)
Heron Park Academy, Eastbourne

Beautiful Minibeast

S lithering slimy snail

N o snail eating

A home to live in

I am safe

L onely, sad snail.

Ari Delapp (6)
Heron Park Academy, Eastbourne

Little Black Spider

S pider looking for food

P lants are yummy

I n the web

D o you like spiders?

E at those spiders, no, no, no!

R ight now!

Zaq Roonan Saquilon Villegas (7)
Heron Park Academy, Eastbourne

Find Out About Some Amazing Minibeasts

S lippery, slimy and slow

N o birds can eat this home

A home to live in

I am scared about living alone

L ong time to move.

Amy Gough (7)
Heron Park Academy, Eastbourne

Rabbit

R abbits are beautiful

A nd they love to hop

B aby rabbits are called kittens

B ig fluffy rabbits

I love my rabbit

T wo rabbits like to play with each other.

Erynn Louise Baxter (6)
Kingswood Primary School, Tadworth

Badger

B adgers are stinky

A white and black little animal

D irty because he digs

G rey fur on his back

E very badger is shy

R ed little ears.

Beau William Best (5)
Kingswood Primary School, Tadworth

Rabbit

R abbits are cuddly

A mazing and talented

B unnies are beautiful

B ouncing bunnies are bouncing

I love bunnies

T he baby rabbits are called kittens.

Toby Love (6)
Kingswood Primary School, Tadworth

Butterfly

B utterflies are beautiful

U sually very pretty

T hey are great at flying

T ruly amazing colours

E xcellent at finding flowers

R ainbow-coloured wings

F loating and fluttering in the sky

L ittle cocoons waiting to turn into butterflies

Y ellow daffodils are their favourite.

Ciara Ella Fall (6)
Kingswood Primary School, Tadworth

Rabbits

R abbits are the best things!

A mazingly good at being nice

B aby rabbits are called kittens

B aby rabbits are so cute

I s so playful

T hey like playing with people.

Charlie Vodden (6)
Kingswood Primary School, Tadworth

Butterfly

B utterflies are very beautiful

U sually butterflies are good

T wo butterflies can fly in the sky

T heir wings are orange as the sun

E very day they flutter for flowers

R ed butterflies enjoy racing

F luttering faster than a jet

L ovely little butterflies

Y ellow spots on their wings.

Stanley Goff (6)
Kingswood Primary School, Tadworth

Rabbit

R abbits are really the best

A ll rabbits are cute and friendly

B eautiful rabbits are cute because they are soft

B unnies are really cute

I t loves to eat orange carrots

T im is my pet rabbit.

Thomas Hopkins (6)
Kingswood Primary School, Tadworth

Rabbit

R abbits are beautiful

A rchie is the name of my rabbit

B aby rabbits are called kittens

B eautiful white fur

I love rabbits

T he rabbit is cute.

Jay Robert Gallard (6)
Kingswood Primary School, Tadworth

Rabbits

R abbits are so good with springs in their legs

A rabbit can hop as high as a giant

B eautiful creatures they are

B oing, boing is how they travel

I love them

T heir fur is as soft as silk.

Evie Catherine Latter (6)
Kingswood Primary School, Tadworth

Butterfly

B utterflies are lovely

U sually have colourful wings

T he butterfly has got beautiful colours

T hey like flowers

E very butterfly has got big wings

R ed butterfly

F lying butterfly everywhere

L ow butterfly

Y ellow as the sun.

Harriet Webb (6)
Kingswood Primary School, Tadworth

Rabbits

R abbits are beautiful

A rabbit is soft

B ouncy bunnies

B rown bunnies

I like rabbits

T he rabbits are great.

Reece Stagg (6)
Kingswood Primary School, Tadworth

73

Hedgehog

H edgehogs have spikes as brown as a tree

E very hedgehog has a tiny grey nose so they can smell lots of wiggly worms

D ifficult to see in the black gloomy dark woods

G reen grass to chew on and colourful leaves to sleep in

E ven cuter than a black and white cat

H edgehogs live inside a long lumpy log

O scar is my hedgehog's name

G orgeous light brown face like a brown dog.

Ruby Barfoot (6)
Kingswood Primary School, Tadworth

Rabbit

R abbits are cute and cuddly

A rabbit springs high

B aby rabbits are called kittens

B unnies are nice

I have a pet rabbit

T he rabbit is lovely.

Sebastian Valentine Best (5)
Kingswood Primary School, Tadworth

74

Rabbit

R abbits are cute because they are little!

A rabbit is grey and fluffy and cuddly!

B unnies can jump really high!

B eautiful rabbits are lovely!

I like rabbits because they look funny!

T immy the rabbit looks beautiful and amazing!

Leeya Okehie (5)
Kingswood Primary School, Tadworth

Rabbit

R abbits are fluffy as a cloud

A rabbit has long ears

B eautiful rabbits

B aby rabbits are called kittens

I love my pet rabbit

T wo rabbits play with each other.

Daley Brill (6)
Kingswood Primary School, Tadworth

Rabbit

R abbits are cuddly

A mazing rabbits

B eautiful rabbits

B ouncing beautiful bunnies

I love rabbits so much

T he rabbits are fluffy.

Oscar Allen (5)
Kingswood Primary School, Tadworth

Butterfly

B utterflies can fly with their wings

U p in the sky

T hey have beautiful wings

T hey are pretty princesses

E very butterfly can fly brilliantly

R ed butterflies are my favourite

F lying butterflies in the garden

L onely pretty butterflies

Y esterday I saw a butterfly.

Penelope Shroll (6)
Kingswood Primary School, Tadworth

76

Squirrels

S quirrels have a very bushy brown tail

Q uickly squirrels climb up trees

U nder the dark brown logs they find acorns to eat

I love squirrels a lot because they are cute

R eally good runners as fast as a cheetah

R ed squirrels are beautiful to look at because they are a burning red colour

E mily was the squirrel's name

L ots of squirrels live in the wild woods.

Megan Filer (6)
Kingswood Primary School, Tadworth

Rabbit

R abbits are so cute because they are cuddly

A rabbit is fluffy

B rilliant rabbits

B ouncy rabbits, like springs

I love my rabbit so, so much

T he rabbit's ears are very long.

Kylah Cemal (5)
Kingswood Primary School, Tadworth

Hedgehog

H edgehogs have spikes as pointy as a thistle which is growing
on the ground
E ndearing cute face on its body
D rinks see-through blue water when it's thirsty
G reat soft fur on its head, like a bunny
E ven cuter than a puppy and a kitten
H edgehogs like green grass and green leaves
O rdinary black and blue eyes on her
G eorgia is my hedgehog's name.

Nadia Hawley (6)
Kingswood Primary School, Tadworth

Rabbits

R abbits are the best
A rabbit's ears are long
B eautiful rabbits
B ouncing rabbits
I love my pet rabbits
T wo rabbits like to play.

Maisie Bough (6)
Kingswood Primary School, Tadworth

Rabbit

R abbits are the best

A rabbit's ears are long

B eautiful rabbit

B ouncy bunny

I like my pet rabbit

T wo rabbits like to play together.

Aiden John Pulham (5)
Kingswood Primary School, Tadworth

Beanstalk

B ig beanstalk growing

E xcitedly Jack climbed up the beanstalk

A xes are sharp

N ew green leaves

S aw really big leaves

T ree is really big

A nts are on the ground

L azy boy

K ind Jack.

Corey White (8)
New Marston Primary School, Oxford

Egg And The Beanstalk

B ig
E gg
A mazing
N arrow
S quiggly
T all
A bove
L ong
K nock.

Zakira Hussain (6)
New Marston Primary School, Oxford

Bean

B eans are magic
E nemies are giants
A mazing beanstalk
N aughty boy.

Maatik Badli-Zonta (6)
New Marston Primary School, Oxford

Beanstalk

B oy

E njoy himself

A nd is a joker

N ame of a person

S at down and ate

T hey play in the garden

A clever boy hid in the cupboard

L ike someone

K ite going up.

Nitara Navin (7)
New Marston Primary School, Oxford

Beanstalk

B eans make plants

E normous beanstalks

A ngry giants

N asty giants

S tinky breath

T all men

A xe

L ittle children

K ids screaming.

Damien Wills (7)

New Marston Primary School, Oxford

Egg And The Beanstalk

B ig
E gg
A mazing
N arrow
S trong
T all
A bove
L eafy
K nock.

Kaleb Davenport (6)
New Marston Primary School, Oxford

Beanstalk

B eanstalk grew up to the sky

E normous beanstalk with big leaves

A nd nosy Jack stole things from the giant

N ever take my treasure, the giant

S aid

T ell me why you stole my treasure

A nd the giant was really angry

L oudly Jack screamed

K illed the giant on the green grass.

Jenaya Hall-Williams (7)
New Marston Primary School, Oxford

Beanstalk

B eanstalk has grown

E normous beanstalk

A nd tall and thin

N aughty Jack why are you climbing me?

S ad and hurt

T aking stuff

A nd running down me

L aughing Jack

K illed the giant on the floor.

Sana Sahonta (6)
New Marston Primary School, Oxford

Beanstalk

B eanstalk
E xciting adventure
A nd leaves touching Heaven
N osy Jack climbed the beanstalk
S trong beanstalk
T he leaves were golden
A ngry beanstalk
L ifeless
K illed.

Alexander Joshua Sydamah Barbosa (7)
New Marston Primary School, Oxford

My Beanstalk

B umpy and soft

E normous and grand

A s fat as an elephant

N o leaf too small or too big!

S o the beanstalk is tallest of all

T all and gigantic

A very vast and tall stalk

L eafy and long

K nocking off leaves and shouting, 'Watch out below!'

Josie Gibbons (7)
New Marston Primary School, Oxford

87

Huge Stalk

B eans are yummy, better for your tummy

E at, eat, eat them up

A n orange bean, a green bean

N ever ever try a bean

S it on a bean please

T alk to me, talk to me

A xe, axe, chop it down

L ike a proper axe, proper axe

K ill him, kill him.

Ellie Hay (7)
New Marston Primary School, Oxford

Beanstalk Poem

B umpy beanstalk

E ven gigantic beanstalk

A long beanstalk

N o the leaves are heavy

S o the beanstalk is a curly

T all beanstalk

A green long beanstalk

L eaves are a step

K ick out half of the leaves.

Eshal Anas (6)
New Marston Primary School, Oxford

Egg And The Beanstalk

B ig
E ggs
A mazing
N arrow
S quiggly
T rembled
A bove
L eafy
K nock.

Maisey Stothard (7)
New Marston Primary School, Oxford

Beanstalk

B is for beanstalks they are noisy in the

E vening

A nd slimy but

N early as tall as a castle

S tairs made of brick

T o break them like a rock

A nd a hard metal chair

L ook but the metal chair is not breaking but the

K ettle is.

Hajra Mahmood (7)
New Marston Primary School, Oxford

Beanstalk

B eanstalk leaves grow through the fresh air

E normous beanstalk, climb if you dare

A nd no one climbed the beanstalk, phew!

N o, someone is climbing the beanstalk, but who?

S omeone got some money

T o be rich to buy some honey

A little beanstalk creaking

L ike the little beanstalk

K ill me, kill me Jack.

Kareem Mohamed Sulaiman (7)
New Marston Primary School, Oxford

The Tall Beanstalk

B eanstalks are very big

E ven the beanstalk is bigger than the clouds

A beanstalk is leafy and green

N ot very light but a bit dark

S o green like a tree

T all beanstalks can be taller than the clouds

A beanstalk is so curvy

L ike climbing a thing

K now how to get the beanstalk growing.

Cameron Williams (7)
New Marston Primary School, Oxford

Snow Leopards

S hh says Mummy, stay in one place so you are camouflaged against the snow

N ow they are big they can roam around free

O h yummy food, Mummy says when she sees a hare

W hen it's winter Daddy says to his cubs, 'Have a little nap.'

L eopards have claws in paws like winter gloves

E veryone needs to care for them

O h help! The family cry when hunters come.

P lease stay calm people should say when they see the scared big cats

A re you OK? asks Mummy when they are left alone

R eally am I seeing a nightmare? He says when he sees his predators

D o your best at being still, says Mummy

S o now the leopards are finally safe.

Jenny Rose Townsend (7)
Oakfield Primary School, Southampton

Dolphins

D ives deep

O cean creature

L ikes fish

P lays in the waves

H ides in the sea

I ntelligent and clever

N ose is short

S prays water.

Estela Hernandez Hernandez Smith (7)
Oakfield Primary School, Southampton

Rabbit

R eally fast runner

A muncher

B rilliant hopper

B eautiful animal

I have long ears

T eeth are sharp.

Rebecca Bundy (7)
Oakfield Primary School, Southampton

Lewis

L ewis is a slow and cheerful boy

E very day I love to play football

W hen I wake up I get ready for school

I n the morning my mummy has to wake me sometimes

S ometimes I have pain au chocolat for breakfast.

Lewis Maughan (7)
Oakfield Primary School, Southampton

Kenny

K enny is cooler than cool ice

E pic friends play with me

N o one is nasty to me

N ow I play Minecraft

Y ou are fantastic.

Kenny Biss (7)
Oakfield Primary School, Southampton

Rhaianna-Mai

R unning around I do quite often

H air I've got is very dark brown

A pples are ripe but I don't like the taste of them

I like crafting things

A meilia my foster sister is adorable, she does not like strawberries and neither do I!

N ibbling squirrels I like watching

N aming birds I like doing

A brother I have, called Taelan Monteiro

M unching on ripe red grapes I love doing

A corns I like planting

I don't like peaches.

Rhaianna-Mai Monteiro (6)
Oakfield Primary School, Southampton

Sloths

S leepy and slow

L eaning down a tree

O versized claws

T otally awesome and cute

H owever they are my favourite animal

S ilvery fur.

Nina Isaac (7)
Oakfield Primary School, Southampton

Meerkat

M y favourite

E verybody loves me because I'm a baby

E verybody protects me from being squashed

R un, danger, danger!

K ill our enemies once and for all

A ll my life I have been snuggled up to friends and family

T all and brave, fearless and friendly, I'm a little tiny meerkat!

Bethany Bluebell Carter-Walsh (6)
Oakfield Primary School, Southampton

Isabelle

I am independent

S uch a gorgeous and smiley girl

A lways crazy and happy

B right

E nergetic

L oving

L ively

E asily impressed.

Isabelle Grace Whalley (7)
Oakfield Primary School, Southampton

Dolphin

D olphins are the best because they are creative

O n the top of the blue sea they splash

L ight on the water they play

P yramid mountains in the distance

H igh in the sky they leap to the clouds

I n the sea they play

N ice dolphins like the sparkling blue sea

S inging dolphins with their wonderful squeak.

Jasmine White (6)
Oakfield Primary School, Southampton

99

Plane

P lanes have great names

L anding a plane is very hard

A plane always has to ask the air control if the road is clear

N o planes have wing mirrors

E xcept my plane.

Isaac Price (7)
Oakfield Primary School, Southampton

My Dog Berry

M ice are horrible animals and my dog eats them

Y ou love to pick up sticks

D odging is fantastic

O reos, Berry likes them

G reat fun to be with her

B all games are fun

E ating biscuits

R unning and chasing

R acing and rolling

Y ummy treats.

Evie Jane-Norman (7)
Oakfield Primary School, Southampton

Singing Star

S inging is for regenerating your voice

I t will make you so famous that you will blow your mind!

N eed to sing on the ultimate X Factor!

G oing to church for someone that has died

I t makes you feel better with a lovely lullaby

N o need to cry, super star is here so there's no fear!

G ot a good voice be a star then!

S trange on stage they might be there for you, just you, for my power of relations are here to cheer for me

T oppings for a delicious cake, come and grab a microphone not a cake!

A re you all in a competition play? Let your voice go among the others!

R otating around the country for them to hear.

Lily May Catherine Tiller (7)
Oakfield Primary School, Southampton

Angel

A ngel is a cute and funny girl

N ew cool boys, cool girls

G irls are good and smelly

E ggs are stinky and weird

L ook! I found a cool pair of trainers and they're cool.

Angel Crystal Heart Fulford (7)
Oakfield Primary School, Southampton

Elephant

E normous huge ears that are baggy

L ong trunks that suck up water and blow it out

E xtended white tusks hanging from my mouth

P ointy tail that is short and smooth

H appily tramping all over the really hot land

A wesome plants to crunch and chew on

N oisy loud sound it makes

T errific thing it is.

Rosie Leeson (6)
Oakfield Primary School, Southampton

Panda

M ummy got a panda
Y ou like pandas

L ove pandas, I do too
O ur panda goes to bed
V ery cuddly as well
E ven I cuddled her at night
L ove pandas, I love you too
Y es I say when I go home

P anda likes me
A nd cuddles me
N ice panda
D ays of cuddling
A fairy came to cuddle her.

Skye Jean Reilly (5)
Our Lady's Preparatory School, Crowthorne

Dinosaurs

D inosaurs are awesome, I like them so much

I guanodon had a spike on his thumb

N edoceratops had a spiky nose

O rnithomimus was a speedy thief

S pino had a spine, he always liked to kill

A patosaurus like munching trees

U tahraptor liked to kill

R ebbachisaurus liked eating plants

S inraptor like munching meat.

William Newman (5)
Our Lady's Preparatory School, Crowthorne

Romans

R omans fight to get more land

O ne day a new soldier came

M onday he went to battle

A fter that he went to another battle

N eeding help

S uddenly he fell to the ground.

Joshua McAllister (6)
Our Lady's Preparatory School, Crowthorne

104

Months

M onday begins with M for May and March

O ut children go trick or treating in October

N ovember there are fireworks

T eachers teach in all the months

H onestly children are excited in December, it's Christmas

S ad people, are sad in January.

Natasha Jastrzebska (6)
Our Lady's Preparatory School, Crowthorne

Dinosaurs

D inosaurs are awesome

I play with my dinosaur Eric

N ature is nice for dinosaurs

O ceans are good for dinosaurs

S tegosaurus is super

A pril I get my dinosaur out

U tahraptor is a small dinosaur

R obot dinosaurs are cool

S tegosaurus swims fast.

Julia Cano (5)
Our Lady's Preparatory School, Crowthorne

Holidays

H elped her dad to make something on holiday

O i that's my coin

L ike the lollipop game

I am hot, can I have an ice cream please?

D ad can I help you?

A ctivities to play

Y ay, this is a cool game

S nakes and ladders, let's go play there.

Phoebe Beaumont (6)
Our Lady's Preparatory School, Crowthorne

Seaside

S easide, seaside, sunny seaside

E very shell I see I will collect

A sandcastle has been knocked down

S easides are really fun

I love the bright sun

D id you see the big boat?

E ven after we dug the sand.

Oliver Rhone (6)
St Bernadette's Catholic Primary School, Farnborough

106

Seaside

S ummer fun

E ating ice cream

A t the seaside

S plashing about

I n the sea

D onkey rides

E very day happy as can be.

Emily Lynch (6)
St Bernadette's Catholic Primary School, Farnborough

Seaside

S easide, seaside we are going to the seaside

E veryone get your bucket and spade

A ll aboard the train, hooray!

S mell the sea, we are nearly there

I ce cream on the sandy beach

D ig a hole in the sand and bury Dad

E veryone had the best day at the seaside.

Millie Lee (6)
St Bernadette's Catholic Primary School, Farnborough

Seaside

S ea and sand
E ven a band
A way up in the sky
S eagulls fly
I ce cream is grand
D igging in the sand
E nd of the land.

Connor Newell (7)
St Bernadette's Catholic Primary School, Farnborough

A Day At The Seaside

S un is shining so let's play today
E very day is fun because there's no excuse not to have fun
A t the seaside let's all be filled with joy
S un keeps shining and keeps me smiling
I ce cream what a treat!
D elicious things to eat that are so sweet
E njoyable day it was, exciting memories to treasure and
    share.

Hannah Oluwatitomi Gbadamosi (7)
St Bernadette's Catholic Primary School, Farnborough

Seaside

S easide, seaside, silly seaside

E ating ice cream

A s cold as ice

S unshine shimmering like a jewel

I n the water nice and cool

D ancing on the sand

E njoying the sun.

Daisy Catherine Southin (6)
St Bernadette's Catholic Primary School, Farnborough

Seaside

S easide, seaside, I love the seaside

E ager to play in the sand

A lot of people along the seaside

S andcastles can only be made by people

I ce cream van we love

D igging sand to make a castle

E veryone loves the seaside.

Paul Andrew Uychocde Jalandra (7)
St Bernadette's Catholic Primary School, Farnborough

Seaside

S eagulls are flying

E njoying the sun

A ll the people are happy

S wimming in the sea

I am eating ice cream

D ogs have fun at the beach

E xploring at the beach.

Will Rhodes (6)
St Bernadette's Catholic Primary School, Farnborough

Chocolate

C hocolate is yummy as hot chocolate

H ot as hot chocolate

O pening wrapping paper makes me excited

C hocolate disturbs me when I'm doing my homework

O range chocolate

L ovely chocolate

A pple chocolate

T offee chocolate

E ating chocolate is my favourite.

Alyanna Leanne Sandagon (5)
St Bernadette's Catholic Primary School, Farnborough

110

Thor

T hunder is his power

H aving a special hammer

O din is his father

R unning away to Earth

M jolinir is his hammer's name

I ntelligence helps him fight

G reatness is in him

H atred never comes to him

T wenty years old

Y ounger brother Loki wants to get rid of him.

Joseph Harrison (7)
St Bernadette's Catholic Primary School, Farnborough

Seaside

S ea waving up and down and side to side

E normous whales in the wavy sea

A dults building sandcastles

S eagulls flying in the air collecting food

I ce cream at the seaside

D igging deep to build the best sandcastles

E verybody loves going to the seaside.

Amelia Dixon (7)
St Bernadette's Catholic Primary School, Farnborough

Ella McCullen

E lla loves chocolate

L ightning scares me

L ove is in my heart

A ccidents happen to me a lot

M ilk is good for me

C akes are yummy for me

C omputer games are fun

U mbrella rhymes with Ella

L ight wakes me up

L ove comes from my mum to me

E venings make me sleepy

N ew clothes come to me a lot.

Ella McCullen (6)
St Bernadette's Catholic Primary School, Farnborough

Football

F ootball is the best game for boys

O n FIFA 15 you get to create your own team and try to win

O ften you get frustrated because you lose the final

T alking to people at half-time is sometimes fun, you get to know how they're feeling

B eginning the season is sometimes scary

A fter you begin the second half it is not really scary

L ater no one will probably score

L ater at the end is very exciting because you get the score.

Fraser Clare (7)
St Bernadette's Catholic Primary School, Farnborough

Summer

S ummer is the time to play and have fun

U nfair, mean and sad, no one should cry in summer

M usic is in summer, when I swim I hear music

M e eating lollipops in the sun

E veryone loves the sunshine

R ound the big swimming pool with my family.

Ava May Todd (6)
St Bernadette's Catholic Primary School, Farnborough

Baseball

B atting the ball is very fun

A ll my family comes to see me

S ometimes I win the game

E ating time is half-time

B ad players are not in the game

A ngry players don't win

L ight of the sun makes the ball shine

L oving players don't stop playing the game.

Kevin Gurung (7)
St Bernadette's Catholic Primary School, Farnborough

114

Monkey

M onkeys are cheeky

O rdinary monkeys eat yellow bananas

N aughty monkeys never stop playing jokes

K issing monkeys is so much fun

E arly in the morning monkeys eat bananas

Y awning monkeys go to bed.

Sarwan Uddin (6)
St Bernadette's Catholic Primary School, Farnborough

Minecraft

M inecraft is fun when I'm with my friends

I n Minecraft I mine and create

N oisy creepers in the night

E mpty, dark, dangerous, deep caves

C reepers creeping behind you at night

R ails under minecarts

A dventures every day

F ast cheetahs running

T he zombies creeping outside.

Myles Connett (7)
St Bernadette's Catholic Primary School, Farnborough

Summer

S ummer is a super season!

U nexpected brilliant surprises

M agical days at the beach

M ad chases, funny times!

E ating delicious scoops of ice cream

R unning around having a race, now it's time to end the day!

Hanako Phillips (7)
St Bernadette's Catholic Primary School, Farnborough

Seaside

S eagulls are as white as snow

E veryone is sitting on the bright golden sand

A lways people swim in the sea

S easide beaches are the places to go

I ce cream is yummy for my tummy

D ancing near the shore makes me want to roar

E veryone enjoys the seaside so much.

Millie Bailey (7)
St Bernadette's Catholic Primary School, Farnborough

Batman

B atman is very helpful and cool

A ction-packed he catches baddies

T aking gadgets to fight

M aybe he's good and runs very fast

A ctivity he does is catching baddies

N ice he is and very brave.

Aleksander Bykowski (6)
St Bernadette's Catholic Primary School, Farnborough

Cats

C ats scratch sofas

A nd they run around

T asty treats for cats

S oft paws to walk.

Izabela Waniowski (5)
St Erme with Trispen Community Primary School, Truro

Dogs

D ogs bark at cats

O utside dogs like to play

G o and get a bone

S troking the dogs is nice.

Ethan Bauer (5)
St Erme with Trispen Community Primary School, Truro

Cats

C heeky cats

A ll cats sleep inside

T asty treats for cats

S cratch dogs.

Jayden Ian Hopkins (6)
St Erme with Trispen Community Primary School, Truro

Koalas

K oalas munch on juicy eucalyptus leaves

O ne baby koala can go on the mummy's back

A koala has sharp claws so they can climb humongous trees

L ike sleeping twenty hours each day

A lways saving energy.

Emma Prowse (6)
St Erme with Trispen Community Primary School, Truro

Koalas

K oalas have sharp claws like needles

O n their heads they have grey fur

A koala can jump tree to tree

L azy koalas sleep in trees

A ll koalas are so lazy because they have sharp claws.

Connor Hayes (7)
St Erme with Trispen Community Primary School, Truro

Amazing Kangaroos

K angaroos munch on crunchy green leaves and water plants

A nimals with pouches are called marsupials

N umber of groups are so much larger than our family

G ood thing about kangaroos, they kickbox

A mazing thing about kangaroos is that brave bucks can fight

R un so fast you can't catch your little legs up

O ften kangaroos swim in deep Australia

O nly eat plants, they're a herbivore.

Ella Ann Nankivell (7)
St Erme with Trispen Community Primary School, Truro

Kangaroo

K angaroos munch on the crunchy trees

A nd tasty plants that are huge

N aked baby kangaroos go in the mum's pouch

G ood things are that they are so fast

A mazing kangaroos are amazing at running

R unning kangaroos run so fast like an aeroplane

O nly kangaroos are called marsupials

O nly baby kangaroos go in a pouch.

Alisha Trythall-Hayes (7)
St Erme with Trispen Community Primary School, Truro

Kangaroo

K angaroos have a pouch to keep their small babies safe

A nd can jump three times their height

N ext they munch on crunchy herbs

G rand kangaroos have very soft skin

A lso kangaroos have a tail to balance

R acing like a racing car

O nly kangaroos can't walk back

O rdinary kangaroos can swim.

Brooke Masters (7)
St Erme with Trispen Community Primary School, Truro

Koala

K oala eats their mummy's dirty pap

O ften koalas sleep in flapping trees

A lways eat hard eucalyptus

L egs are furry and grey

A lways koalas grip hard onto swishing trees.

Hollie Treloar (6)
St Erme with Trispen Community Primary School, Truro

Platypus

P latypuses sunbathing like little soft babies next to the blue rushing river

L ush brown fur slithering through your fingers

A ny platypus is grabbing nice juicy fish to grind up

T he platypuses are probably curling up their tails and curling up next to the babies

Y our platypus has a rubbery bill like a bird

P robably the soft babies are snuggling up to the mother

U seless for being naughty as they sunbathe under the sun

S ome people long ago thought they were made-up creatures.

Katie Smiles (7)
St Erme with Trispen Community Primary School, Truro

Goanna

G oannas have black and white scales

O n their lumpy backs

A goanna lays white eggs in a crumbly termite mound

N ervous goannas sense with their tongues

N ext goannas devour crunchy scorpions

A goanna never gets poisoned.

Callum Penrose (5)
St Erme with Trispen Community Primary School, Truro

Amazing Kangaroos

K angaroos jump higher than tall grass and

A s they jump their tail helps them to balance

N o kangaroos kill things

G laring sun shines on the kangaroo's furry back

A s they are born the mum bleeds

R eally good kangaroos won't fight but bucks do

O ozing babies come from their mum's tummy

O ften kangaroos take a swim.

Zinnia Porter (7)
St Erme with Trispen Community Primary School, Truro

Koala Crazy

K oala has funny, amazing skin like a purring cat

O rdinary koalas eat stinky pap

A lways clinging onto towering tall trees

L eaning koalas transport tiny babies in soft pouches

A re clever marsupials which have a powerful jump.

Noah Martin (7)
St Erme with Trispen Community Primary School, Truro

Koala

K oalas are amazing and brilliant

O ne koala has a pouch and they eat their mummy's pap

A ll baby cubs have soft bellies

L azy koalas sleep for twenty hours

A koala is soft like a teddy.

Jessica Tierney (6)
St Erme with Trispen Community Primary School, Truro

Lazy Crocodiles

C heeky crocodiles live underwater

R esting in the bright sun crocodiles lie

O nly chase food then drown them

C rocodiles are crunching fish

O nly crocodiles can hear their eggs underground

D o not go near crocodiles

I think they're bumpy but smooth on their tummies

L eave them alone or else they will eat you

E very crocodiles lies underwater with eyes and nostrils out.

Evie Grace Hawkins (6)
St Erme with Trispen Community Primary School, Truro

Koala

K oalas have joeys in pouches

O nly climb up trees when they are grown up

A nd mummy koalas feed joeys

L ook after your joey koala

A nd koalas slide them in their soft pouches.

Jazmine Bellamy (5)
St Erme with Trispen Community Primary School, Truro

Silly Goanna

G oannas are reptiles

O n the gold sand

A nd they climb up trees

N ext they eat scorpions

N ever poison a goanna

A nd they have a tongue to sense human predators.

Alfred George James (6)
St Erme with Trispen Community Primary School, Truro

Koalas

K oalas jump from tree to tree fast

O n their furry backs when climbing trees are their small babies

A baby koala is called a joey

L azy koalas sleep twenty hours

A furry koala has a fluffy pouch

S mall baby koalas eat special pap.

Austin Rowe (6)
St Erme with Trispen Community Primary School, Truro

Koala

K oalas grip onto lush trees

O ften koala babies spend all their time eating pap

A lways they spend their time sleeping loudly

L onely koalas sleep twenty hours a day

A gain koalas munching rock-hard eucalyptus leaves.

Alfie Jones (6)
St Erme with Trispen Community Primary School, Truro

Cheeky Koalas

K oalas have sharp claws so they can climb high trees

O n backs

A ll baby koalas are in the soft pouch eating amazing milk

L azy koalas sleep up to twenty hours

A mummy koala chews lots of eucalyptus leaves.

Abi Wallace (6)
St Erme with Trispen Community Primary School, Truro

Goanna Crazy

G o careful goannas eat anything

O range goannas are like fire burning

A very harmful predator

N oisy when they gallop across the hot sand

N aughty goannas eat crunchy scorpions

A nimals are afraid of it.

Alfie Dowson (7)
St Erme with Trispen Community Primary School, Truro

Goannas

G oannas run fast on the ground because the sand is hot

O nly when they are hungry they eat a scorpion and it won't sting

A nd they dig

N ext they will not eat

N ext it will walk away

A nimals run fast like goannas.

Aimee Martin (5)
St Erme with Trispen Community Primary School, Truro

Hedgehog

H ungry

E xcellent

D ark brown

G reat

E yes that are blue

H ungry

O range spikes

G obbling food.

George McSweeney (6)
The Baird Primary Academy, Hastings

Lion

L is for lovely

I is for incredible

O is for orange fur

N is for nice.

Summer Bourne-Vagg (5)
The Baird Primary Academy, Hastings

Lion

L is for loud

I is for incredible

O is for orange fur

N is for noisy.

Amelia Fisher (6)
The Baird Primary Academy, Hastings

Lion

L is for lazy

I is for incredible

O is for orange fur

N is for noisy.

James Knapper (6)
The Baird Primary Academy, Hastings

Donkey

D ark grey
O ld
N eeding grass
K ind
E eyore
Y ellow eyes.

Sofia Ivy Lane (6)
The Baird Primary Academy, Hastings

Lion

L is for long tail
I is for incredible
O is for orange fur
N is for noisy and naughty.

Lacey Taylor (6)
The Baird Primary Academy, Hastings

Cat

C is for cute
A is for adorable
T is for twitchy tail.

Jaden Christopher (6)
The Baird Primary Academy, Hastings

Rabbit

R is for run fast
A is for adorable
B is for bouncy
B is for bobby tail
I is for incredible
T is for tickly.

Isis Rees (6)
The Baird Primary Academy, Hastings

Cat

C is for cute and cuddly
A is for adorable
T is for talented.

Jayden Allam (6)
The Baird Primary Academy, Hastings

Dog

D is for diamond
O is for orange nose
G is for growling.

Savannah-Rose Thomas (5)
The Baird Primary Academy, Hastings

Cat

C is for cute
A is for adorable
T is for tiny.

Syena Jardine (6)
The Baird Primary Academy, Hastings

Dog

D is for dark brown fur

O is for orange nose

G is for growling.

Freya Bailey (5)
The Baird Primary Academy, Hastings

Pirate Poem

P irate on the ship

I n with treasure

R ats in the ship

A rms in the water

T he treasure chest

E mpty.

Aiden Parker (5)
Turners Hill CE Primary School, Crawley

Pirate Poem

P arrot on my shoulder
I have a black hat
R um in my tum!
A golden earring
T reasure map blowing
E ye patch and stripy vest.

George Bouck-Standen (5)
Turners Hill CE Primary School, Crawley

Pirate Poem

P irate on the ship
I am fierce
R ed and white stripy shirt
A ye, aye captain
T reasure map
E very pirate has a pirate ship.

Jodie Disa Smith (5)
Turners Hill CE Primary School, Crawley

134

Pirate Poem

P eg leg made of wood

I see a pirate coming

R ats in the ship

A Jolly Roger flying

T hey have got the treasure

E nough to fill the chest.

Miley Bowers (5)
Turners Hill CE Primary School, Crawley

Pirate Poem

P eg leg bang!

I am a pirate

R um in me tum

A ye, aye captain

T reasure chest full

E very pirate needs a hat.

Christopher Bouck-Standen (5)
Turners Hill CE Primary School, Crawley

Pirate Poem

P eg leg banging on the deck

I like treasure

R agged trousers

A parrot on me shoulder

T reasure chest

E arrings, they are round.

Zachary Lucifer Sturgess (5)
Turners Hill CE Primary School, Crawley

Pirate Poem

P arrot on my shoulder

I am a mighty pirate

R um is yum

A ll pirates have a parrot

T aking treasure is what I like

E arrings shining gold.

Hazel Bennett (4)
Turners Hill CE Primary School, Crawley

Pirate Poem

P irate on a ship, pirate overboard

I like being a pirate, it is fun

R igging is a rope to climb up

A pirate is a person that steals treasure

T he pirate is having a great time

E arrings need holes for the ear.

Mia Simpson (5)
Turners Hill CE Primary School, Crawley

Pirate Poem

P irate has a fluffy beard

I have a sword in my pocket

R ats! All over the ship

A ll pirates have rum

T en pirates can be on the ship

E arrings and coins and crowns in the treasure chest.

Nathanael Jozef Leslie (5)
Turners Hill CE Primary School, Crawley

Super Stephen

S awing Stephen

T urning wheels

E nergetic exercise

P inging springs

H andsome prince

E xciting ideas

N ice son.

Stephen Connolly (6)
Wildground Infant School, Southampton

Funny Freyja

F rightened because I hate the dark

R ock star because I like pop music

E xcited because I like school trips

Y esterday I went to the park

J affa cakes are my favourite

A mazing at riding my bike.

Freyja Smyth (6)
Wildground Infant School, Southampton

Amazing Asifa

A mazing because my friends tell me

S hy, I am embarrassed

I ndependent, I do things by myself

F riendly because I like to be kind to my friends

A beautiful girl, my friends tell me I am.

Asifa-Almas Mian (6)
Wildground Infant School, Southampton

Curious Cole

C are, I help people

O dd, I love being different

L ong, I am tall

E xcellent, I am brilliant at music.

Cole Austin Doak (6)
Wildground Infant School, Southampton

139

Silly Sophie

S parkle, my hair is glittery

O range, it is my favourite colour

P retty, I have a pretty smile

H appy, I am always smiling

I ntelligent, I am always right

E ntertaining, I love shows.

Sophie Evans (6)
Wildground Infant School, Southampton

Noisy Connor

C hatterbox because I always chatter

O dd because I grew up

N ormal because I am the same

N aughty because I don't do tidying

O range is the colour of the rainbow

R ock star because I like noise.

Connor John Weafer (6)
Wildground Infant School, Southampton

Silly Joe

J oking, I do my best jokes
O ranges are my favourite fruit
E xcellent, I do my best.

Joseph Adhikary (6)
Wildground Infant School, Southampton

Annoying Daniel

D ogs are lovely
A nxious when I write
N ice because I am nice to everyone
I nto bed to get some rest
E ating cake is my favourite
L ove my class.

Daniel Wheeler-Osman (6)
Wildground Infant School, Southampton

Cool Cody

C ool, I'm cool because I read properly

O range, I like the colour orange

D ressing up, I love dressing up as Elsa

Y oung, I'm young because I'm little.

Cody Willsher (5)
Wildground Infant School, Southampton

Quiet Shaun

S hort hair

H appy smile

A dventurous games

U ntidy bedroom

N ibbling apples.

Shaun Yeates (6)
Wildground Infant School, Southampton

Foxy Jordon

J uggling carrots
O dd socks
R unning fast
D isco mouse
O range trainers
N ibbling cake.

Jordon Harris (5)
Wildground Infant School, Southampton

Kind Kenzie

K ind
E arly
N eat
Z ooming
I ncy
E xcitable.

Kenzie Copper (5)
Wildground Infant School, Southampton

Funny Alicia

A pple eating

L ovely hair

I cy cold

C limbing a rope

I mportant writing

A mazing painting

M agic sparkling nails

A cting Elsa

Y oung face.

Alicia-May Rogers (6)
Wildground Infant School, Southampton

Zooming Zach

Z is for zooming everywhere

A is for awesome because I'm the class joker

C is for being cool because I wear my hat back to front

H is for being happy because I have a big smile on my face.

Zachary Colley-Grant (6)
Wildground Infant School, Southampton

Jessica

J oker because I tell jokes

E xcited because I'm on holiday

S illy, I do silly dances

S weet because I am kind

I ndependent, I work on my own

C lever, I like maths

A mbitious, I want to be a policewoman.

Jessica Hindson (6)
Wildground Infant School, Southampton

Marvellous Megan

M is for being marvellous at school

E is for being energetic always

G is for being grateful with good manners

A is for amazing, I'm good wherever I go

N is for being nice to everyone.

Megan Davison (6)
Wildground Infant School, Southampton

Resourceful Ruby

R is for resourceful, clever and smart
U is for understanding, being kind to my friends
B is for bouncing high in the sky
Y is for yo-yo, make it go down and up.

Ruby Rose Cross (6)
Wildground Infant School, Southampton

Alesha Hall

A is for ambitious
L is for lovely
E is for excellent
S is for smiley
H is for happy
A is for athletic.

Alesha Hall (5)
Wildground Infant School, Southampton

Amazing, Clever Aissa

A is for being astonishing because I am

I is for being intelligent because I am clever in maths

S is for being smiley all day long

S is for smartie pants all the time

A is for being awesome all the time.

Aissa Parfitt (5)
Wildground Infant School, Southampton

Amazing Ella

E is for energy, I have lots of it

L is for laughing all the time

L is for lovely, I'm a good friend

A is for amazing, I'm good at school.

Ella Sandy (5)
Wildground Infant School, Southampton

Toby The Terrific

T errific, I work hard
O utstanding, I am helpful
B rilliant at being good
Y oung, I'm full of energy.

Toby Reece (5)
Wildground Infant School, Southampton

Super Sam

S is for super all day long
A is for awesome at karate
M is for marvellous, diving at great heights.

Sam Kneller-Hole (6)
Wildground Infant School, Southampton

Tegan The Neat

T is for tiger, I will growl if I am angry
E is for energetic, I've got plenty and it makes me run fast
G is for a good friend even if my friend is on another table
A is for apple, it is my favourite food
N is for Nanny, I love her.

Tegan Beavis (6)
Wildground Infant School, Southampton

Nice Katelin

K is for keeping fit, I like doing exercises

A is for astonishing, I'm astonishing at kickboxing

T is for terrific at reading

E is for energy, I'm always on the go

L is for lying. Sometimes I lie at home

I is for independent. I do it by myself

N is for nice. I am nice to people.

Katelin Talisha Hamilton (6)
Wildground Infant School, Southampton

Summer

S is for shy, I don't like talking all day

U is for unusual because I cry when someone says a word

M ischievous because I'm always up to something at home

M is for messing around, I like it

E is for excellent all the time

R is for rubbish at finding things.

Summer Gunter (6)
Wildground Infant School, Southampton

Sophie

S is for smiley

O is for outstanding

P is for polite

H is for happy

I is for intelligent

E is for energetic.

Sophie Muir (6)
Wildground Infant School, Southampton

Delightful Daniella

D is for dinosaur, because I like them a lot

A is for ambitious, I want to be a librarian

N is for nice, because I am kind

I is for independent, I work on my own

E is for energetic, I'm always on the go

L is for lovely, because I'm nice to my friends

L is for learning, I always try my best

A is for amazing, because I am.

Daniella Murrell (5)
Wildground Infant School, Southampton

X-Ray Alex

A is for amazing, I'm always good at school

L is for laughing out loud like a hyena

E is for excellent at reading and writing

X is for X-ray on my poorly leg.

Alex Jennings (6)
Wildground Infant School, Southampton

George Is Bonkers

G reat, I do good work

E ntertaining, I like putting on shows

O dd, I like being different

R ock star, I like listening to cool music

G ood-looking, I like looking cool

E xcitable, I am very bouncy.

George Broom
Wildground Infant School, Southampton

Young Writers Information

We hope you have enjoyed reading this book – and that you will continue to in the coming years.

If you're a young writer who enjoys reading and creative writing, or the parent of an enthusiastic poet or story writer, do visit our website **www.youngwriters.co.uk**. Here you will find free competitions, workshops and games, as well as recommended reads, a poetry glossary and our blog.

If you would like to order further copies of this book, or any of our other titles, then please give us a call or visit **www.youngwriters.co.uk.**

Young Writers,
Remus House,
Coltsfoot Drive,
Peterborough
PE2 9BF.
(01733) 890066 / 898110
info@youngwriters.co.uk